Thank you for choosing "The Book Of Vint
by Pretty Pine Press!

Would you like a **FREE e-BOOK?**

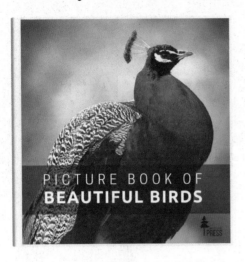

To claim your gift email us at
prettypinepress@gmail.com

WE'D LOVE YOUR FEEDBACK!

★ ★ ★ ★ ★

Please let us know how we are doing
by leaving us a review on Amazon.

PRETTY PINE
PRESS

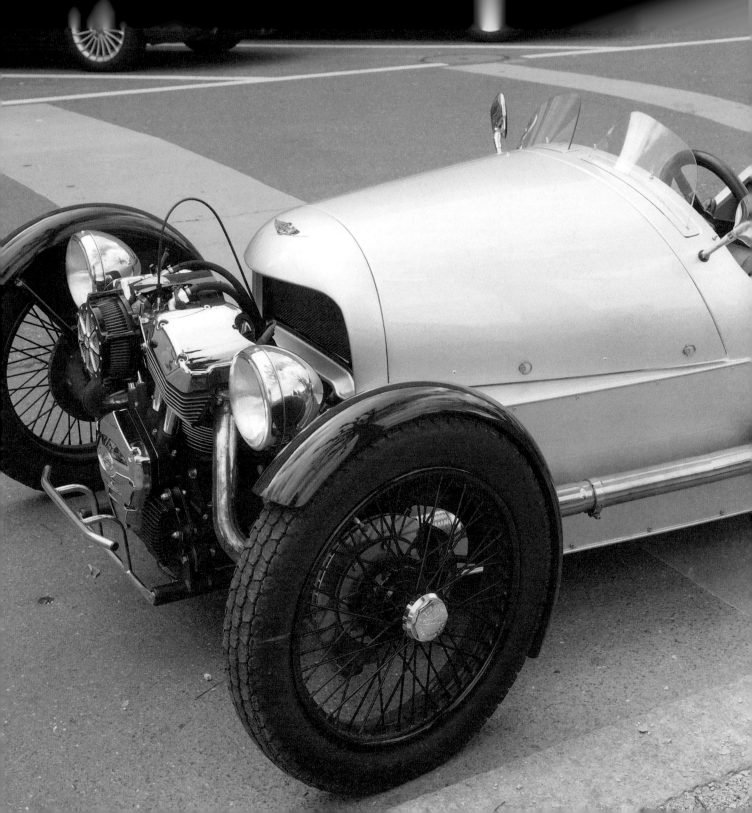